In a

Heart's

Breath

oems by Wendy Negley

In a Heart's Breath

ISBN: 9781948261692
Library of Congress Control Number:
2023905948

Cover & Interior Design: Diane Woods

BANYAN · TREE · PRESS

Published 2023 by Banyan Tree Press,
an imprint of Hugo House Publishers, Ltd.
Denver Colorado, Austin Texas.

DEDICATION

To Dennis and Bill, my two loves

For all the love and support that you have

given me, many thanks. You have given me

the space in which to create the poetry.

CONTENTS

LOVE (of course, what else?)   **101**

AND EVERYTHING ELSE

INTRODUCTION

Here is my next book!

It is a combination of poems I have written since

the last book, earlier ones that didn't make it

into the last book, and poems that I wrote in

High School but had thought lost.

I mentioned to my best friend from High

School, Nancy, that I no longer had the poems I

had written back then. Turned out that I had

made a book of poems for her and she still had

it!

She emailed me the poems. I was amazed at the

similarities of some of them to the ones I've

written recently.

I've included them for your enjoyment and you can see for yourself the comparison between the ones I wrote at 16 and 17 and the ones I wrote at 73—55 years later. Age is an arbitrary, at least when it comes to art.

These poems were written to help me cope with life, to comment on life, to add an aesthetic to life or, frankly, just for fun!

I hope that you enjoy these poems, that they speak to you, that they enhance your life, and, hey!, that you have some fun here, too.

Wendy

Beaverton, Oregon

16 October 2022

IN A HEART'S BREATH   2021

In a heart's breath

I was taken

Past the point

Of thinking twice

Past a point of

Logical reflection

Into a world of

Image feeling action

Where yet no action

Could be done

In one heart's breath

My life was borne

Upon a different line

Almost a new

Dimension

Now would I change

That tide?

Undo that breath?

Go back to how Life was?

The heart doesn't breathe that often

The wise one pays

Utmost attention

When it does.

EARLY POEMS

"Through our great good fortune in our youth, our
hearts were touched with fire."
Oliver Wendell Holmes, Jr.

DEDICATION
FOR A BOOK OF POEMS   1966

Here are our silences

love, not forgotten

I give you our movement

Do not turn

do not turn now from me

for look

here is our

then

(our then was a moving silence

more than your now or my am

can be)

The then your now forgets

Take this

(no longer silent

the movement

stilled)

then.

Do you catch the time of the tune

that the shepherd plays,

The time of the tune he expects

your brain to dance to

The time of the tune as irregular

as the bough?

Catch the time, the time of the tune

Where all sense lies. Feeling the

Halt and flow the flux of speech

Note the movement of hand and eye

And under the hand the quickening pulse.

Hear the beat—here, touch

Is it caught is it felt in your blood, brother?

Here is a strange dance—rhythmic medley

Your diddle my dee intricately woven into dum

And deaf music sings in our veins.

VOLUNTEER PARK: WINTER/SPRING 1966

For Pat

I. The Idols

January 30

The sun shone shyly for your return,

Together we entered the greenhouse.

Eyes dilating in lush darkness

We drank hot colored flowers

On every breath. I wished

To look, but you would hold.

(I'm told when you were young

You kicked the flowers to take a petal home)

Denied the whole, you picked

The fallen petals from the sand

And filled our pockets full.

With care we crept out past the guard,

In mist-grey January afternoon

Our pockets deeply burned with June.

I am not one to take such treasure home

To lie buried in clutters of papers and days.

I saw the idols, forgotten rams of stone,

And ran with burning unburnt offering.

You to one, I to the other

We laid our petals out, plastered

On with wind and rain:

Eyes to the idols, lips to the gods,

Leaving a blur of color in the cold grey day.

II. The Tower

March 24

March was the month we climbed the tower

Round in the dark and the steep stone steps

It was light on the landing, dark on the stair,

You followed close behind me.

The top of the tower was a round of light

We circled slow aglow with sun and sky

The mountains bound our view

But we could see for hours.

The descent and you went first in joy

Running down the stairs. I paused, came

Step by step in fear, trusting neither foot

Nor stair, at each step feeling falling.

The light, the land, the grass at last

Were reached.

We left the tower over gravel walks

Past identical pools and well-laid

Pansy beds and turned the bend.

We met a streak of sleek gray movement

"Is it an otter?" I asked the man at the end

Of the leash. He nodded yes. These were the

Only words and they were mine.

You knelt and stroked the otter's fur.

I could not reach out so, but looked at you,

The otter, the gentleman with sleek gray hair

And said, "Good-bye."

These were the only words, and they were mine.

VENDREDI APRES-MIDI 1966

Le son du violon au salon

Se mele avec les vaiselles du cuisine

Soulignment le bavardage des femmes.

Le violon-seul lien

Des deus femmes qui aiment

Cet homme jouant

Chacune a son facon

Le joueur, sait-il l'amour des femmes?

Est-ce qu'il joue, le jouer,

Pour faire danser leurs coeurs?

Friday Afternoon

The sound of the violin in the salon

Joins with the luncheon china

To emphasize the feminine chatter

The violin alone binds

The two women who love

This man who plays it

Each one in her fashion

The player, does he know of the love of the women?

Is that why he plays, the player,

To make their hearts dance?

WINDBLOWN

I

Yes. The wind roars.

Yes is his sound.

How warm I've grown

In the midst of his cold

Fingers. Discover:

My hair's blown black.

What do I lack?

The wind's my lover.

And all the papers of old

Emotions are blown

Up off the ground.

Yes. My spirit soars.

II

Yes. The wind roars

What do I lack?

Yes is his sound.

The wind's my lover:

How warm I've grown!

And all the papers of old,

In the midst of his cold

Emotions, are blown

Fingers. Discover:

Up off the ground

My hair's blown black

Yes. My spirit soars.

III

Yes. My spirit soars.

Up off the ground

Emotions are blown

And all the papers of old.

The wind's my lover,

What do I lack?

My hair's blown black.

Fingers discover:

In the midst of his cold

How warm I've grown.

Yes is his sound

Yes. The wind roars.

SONG TO BE SUNG IN THE ALLEY   1966

Though it's Spring,

To judge by hours,

I have walking seen

A tree's dead leaves

Unblown, and wind-love

Helpless as the apple sours.

Still, the air is keen.

(And I hear flowers grow.)

What is the flower

Of growing sound?

The fruit of wind-blow

Is the fall of leaf

And when my fingers

Touch the ground,

Then I hear flowers grow.

"Man who must define . . ."   1966

Man who must define

To know, happy

With the content of his hand

Deifies the defined

Defies the divine.

"I am that I am."

Says the burning voice

In the bush.

Man hears with his ears

And (forgetting that) calls this

Jehovah, worships

The stone in his hand

While God slips

Through his fingers

Like the infinite sand.

To PDK

I know a man obsessed by hands;

A poet's soul and quick his touch

Like silver lips. With fingers'

Star-crossed tips he kissed his throaty

Violin. He played the taut, true string

And plucked with fingers made to sing.

He did not play the palm, cupped

To receive, not let himself believe

In Fortune's lines of fame. Ungreased,

He only clasped his palms to praise

His fingers raise the cry beyond his grasp

Ten voiceless longings reach in his handclasp.

And finding joy she gave

And neither suffered nor loved in silence

But poured out her song

Despite the feathers.

She felt the fetters' keen pull

And strained and set against the world

Her own fragility.

And though she shatters

Hope holds her whole.

Her hands hold life whitely, love lightly,

Colors whirl a rainbow roun' her head:

The sun's caught in her hair

While rain falls all around.

FOR NANCY

I will not say

That she was like the daisies

Though she was bright

And fresh enough, it's true:

But not so simple

Yet she was gay

And danced much in the wind

And laughed like rain

Yes, but she sang tunes

No daisy ever knew

And hurled them madly

At the moon.

"The artist along with everyone else ..." *   1966

Not for us Innisfree

No Hermitage retreat

Nor walled-in one (or II)

Shall shelter us from smog.

For we must know and knowing right

Knowing write.

>   (Shall we go then you and I
>
>   When the shadows end the day
>
>   Turn our backs to the firelit sky
>
>   And learn to ride the subway?)

Not for us the lover sea mother

For in this womb the ancient lies

Still borne. Here is no light: no right

Comes forth.

* Saul Bellow on acceptance of the National Book Award

(In the subway we read

People reading newspapers.

From this womb we shall emerge

Rumpled into write light.)

LETTER ON A COLD
DAY IN JULY   1966

It is only because I'm lonely

That I think of you now,

Rain falls like the rain of November.

Love, the madronas are bleeding

Who has torn the bark

From the branches?

Blood of old wounds congeals on the naked wood,

And still the leaves point upward

Their mute cries of green.

Love, for what are they pleading?

The skies and the waters are gray

They are silent and endless.

There are no halls so empty

As these when you are gone,

Nor eyes lonelier.

My inverted love rages at you

Whose absence fills these halls

With aching.

No anger shouts more fury

Than mine when you appear

Smiling.

LEO ASCENDANT IN THE
HOUSE OF CAPRICORN

To M.

It has been a year

And a day

Since you were

Here last:

How well you know

My house.

You stride through

These halls

With leonine pride

As once

You strode through

My heart

And all its red plush rooms.

"Like the sun . . ."   1966

Like the sun

My anger rises

Over the mountains

Fire-round it grows

Like the sun

My anger rises

Burning into the cold

And empty sky

My mind has become

Burning the dark

Shortening shadows

As it climbs

It sears the sky

Bleaching all in

Fierce white light

No shadow

At my anger's height.

SONG

Catch the time of the tune
Of the sun and the moon
Feel the rhyme and the roar
Of the sea and the shore.

Seeing is feeling; feeling's belief
Says the heart of the toad
Says the vein of the leaf.

In the seasonal whirl
In the boy, in the girl
In the rain, in the snow
Where's the sense of the show?

But breathing is telling
And breathing is slow
This rhythmical beating
Is all that we know.

FAMILY ALWAYS

"Family is not an important thing.
It is everything."
Michael J. Fox

FAMILY TREE

Names and dates

And places past

Just ink and dust

As dust they last

And yet I read the stories

Hidden in the tomes

My mind puts flesh

Back on the bones

The records show me

How they lived

This body breathes

Because they loved

They live again

Upon my tree

A kind of

Immortality

Doctor, Minister,

Lawyer,

Chemist,

Carpenter, Farmer,

Barber,

Dentist,

Textile Worker,

Carriage Maker,

Teacher, Vintner,

Undertaker,

Peddler, Seamstress,

Weaver,

Baker, Lineman,

Reiver,

Herb grower, Professor,

Economist,

Stenographer, Secretary,

Pacifist,

Ironmonger, Merchant,

Sailor,

Missionary, Mason,

Tailor,

Lumber jacks,

Drivers of hacks,

Housewives galore,

Soldiers at war,

Textbook writers,

Fiction, too,

Every job under the blue,

But not a poet,

To be found,

Searched my tree

Up and down,

It seems that honor goes to me

Now I can see

What I can be.

ISABELLA

She loved yellow roses

And grew them outside her bay window

So that she could watch them

As she knew she was dying

Their beauty fed her spirit

Filled her soul

A cheerful color to make her smile

A sweet scent to ease her passing

Thorns to remind her

That life is hard

But worth the journey.

I buy yellow roses today

And place them on my table

And think of her

My grandfather's mother

And salute her

She gave beauty, poetry and music

To her children

And they to theirs

And here I am her heir

I put yellow roses on my table

And revel in their beauty.

My great grandfather fought with Sherman

He marched in order to the sea

He burned Atlanta to the ground

He brought the South to her knees

But the swamps of Georgia had revenge

They got into his body and never let go

His body fought but could never make end.

You can bring the South down

In a deep deep hole

But you can't get her dark, dank places

Out of your soul.

"They've forgotten me,"

She whispered.

"No," I said, "No, no they wouldn't.

No one who ever knew you

Could forget you.

They'd remember you!"

"They'd remember you

The way you remember

The beauty of sunrise

Flushed peach and pink

Across the sky."

"They'd remember you

The way they remember

The full moon rising

Huge in the night

Floating on a sil'vry path

Across the bay.

They'd remember you."

The sunrise fades

The moon sets

The breath dies.

But this grace,

This spirit,

This exquisite beauty,

This you,

Goes on.

We'll remember you

And when next we meet,

We'll remember

And rejoice.

For Rhonda

Everyone knows that

Little sisters

Are a pest

They follow you

And bug you

But then they

Go and hug you.

Your friend

Your foe

They won't

Let go.

They just make

You so mad!

But then, they make

You so glad!

Everyone knows that

Little sisters

Are the best.

THE DIVORCE

I saw my Daddy reading Spock

I felt a little bit of shock

Why is he asking for advice?

Haven't I been acting nice?

I'd skipped the chapter that he read

As one that I would never need.

Then they sat us down and said

Their marriage had come to an end.

My rage was hot my rage was true

My rage was what they never knew

We love you both they let us know

As if that would decrease the blow

I felt they broke their word to me

Our family should forever be

My mother was a mass of grief

My father happy with relief

My sister didn't understand

I knew I had to take command

I knew my life was up to me

My family now was all asea

I think my childhood ended there

From that time I was too aware.

FOR MY DAD

I never wrote

His memorial poem

Today it seems

The time has come.

Love made him

Decide to leave,

His wife and children

Left to grieve

He was a good man

Even so

He caused his loved ones

Tears of woe

Years on I started

Down his path

But I could see

The aftermath

And so I wouldn't

Go his way

And so I made

A different play.

 He died a loved

And honored man

And I still honor

What I can.

On him I will not

Place a blame

But, yet I'll never

Do the same.

THIS IS YOUR SON

This is your son, you said,

But this is not my son,

This stranger on the phone,

Not the boy I know.

A stranger by your own choice.

It is your life,

I concede this.

But you are not my son.

(Oh, how I would welcome my son home!)

REQUIEM FOR MY SON   30 OCT 2021

I wish you were dead

A terrible thing for a mother to say

If you were dead, I could mourn you

I could write sweet poems in your honor

I could post cute photos on Facebook

And have everyone admire you

The adorable baby boy

His mother's own heart.

Instead for me, you

No longer exist

Wiped from my life

But I know you live somewhere

As you live in my heart

An open wound, that can't close

I put you from my mind

And live my life

And wonder why I ache.

A boy we thought

We surely knew

A boy whose heart

We thought was true

A boy whose laughter

Made us sing

A boy who happiness

Could bring

He threw himself

Against a wall

And bouncing off

Laughed at the fall

But as he grew

Some changes came

What they were

We couldn't name.

We lost the boy

Who made us smile

We haven't seen him

For awhile.

He's now unknown

In every way

Where he is

We couldn't say

But still our hearts

Say he is known

And still we wish

He could come home.

THE MAN HE HAD TO BE

She looked upon

Her babe, her son

And prayed she could

Help him become

The man he had to be.

She taught him right

Apart from wrong

She taught him how

To sing his song

She gave him love

She gave him truth

And watched for him

To show the proof.

He grew and married

Had a son

Then he showed

He had become

The man he had to be.

DENNIS   28 JAN 2020

Brother

Lover

Father

Friend

We won't

See

Your like

Again

WENDY'S SONG FOR DENNIS: EARTH, WATER & SKY

Stars light up your sky

A lamp that I read by shines over my head

You sail on your ship

While I lie alone in my bed.

CHORUS

Darling, just Earth, Water & Sky

Keep me away from you

Darling, just Earth, Water & Sky

Split our lives in two.

You look at the sea

And smile at the love I bring to your life

I look at the trees

With joy that you've made me your wife.

CHORUS

Often at night when I sleep

I seem to be on some distant shore

Often at night when you sleep

You seem to be back at my door.

CHORUS

You, like so many men

Must battle and conquer the storms of the sea

I, like so many women

Must conquer the time till you come back to me.

CHORUS

Some people who live side by side

Might as well live on opposite shores of the sea

Some people who live side by side

Share less than the love between you and me.

SONG FOR DENNIS   CHRISTMAS, 1992

The years never matter

Time is all lies

Truth is forever

And love never dies.

When first I knew you

You'd just turned a man

Now life has borne on you

As only life can

But when everything else

Has slipped out of my hold

The one thing I know is

Love never grows old.

The years never matter

Time is all lies

Truth is forever

And love never dies.

When you look at me

What do you see?

The girl or the woman

Or the truth that is me?
The surface all changes
Like chalk in the rain
It's all washed away
But still we remain.

The years never matter

Time is all lies

Truth is forever

And love never dies.

LOVE AS LOVE SHOULD BE   20 NOV 2021

For Walter and Bessie

It was love as love should be.

He saw her in her gym outfit

And knew she was the one

She saw him tall and handsome

And knew that she was done

He walked miles to end his promise

To a girlfriend back at home

She argued with her parents

Who thought she was too young.

They married in her Church

For everyone to see

Before their God and family

Their love was meant to be.

They lived through two World Wars

The great Depression, too

With children, then their children

Always coming through

They lived through ban the bomb

And the War in Vietnam

Though the birth of the age of Space

And the death of segregating race

The birth of the internet as well

Through beatniks, hippies,

Peaceniks, yippies

More than they could tell.

At the end the home

In which they were

Put them in separate rooms

That he would have to stir

He got up every day and dressed

And walked across the hall

So he could spend the day with her

He still came to her call

When she died he was bereft

And no more left his bed

When he died, his loved ones

Turned aside and said

"He's gone to join her

Can't you see."

For they had love as love should be.

CHRISTMAS

"Christmas can't be bought from a store
Maybe Christmas means a little bit more."

Dr. Suess

Joy!

{not to the world)

Joy just to me

Also a little

Can be for thee

But mostly,

Joy comes

To me!

Love is

The reason

Throughout

The season

Giving us light

All the long night.

Joy now

To everyone

I must agree

Christmas

For everyone

Not just for me.

JUST A POEM FOR CHRISTMAS 15 DEC 2021

For my husband who doesn't like Christmas

What!

Not like Christmas!

Are you mad?

How can you find

This season so bad?

Now sit beside me

Here on the couch

And stop behaving

 Like a big grouch.

Were you mistreated

When you were a boy

That you can't share

In the season's joy?

See all the presents

Under the tree

You may remember

That giving comes free.

You put the X

In Christmas

You added silent

To the night

You told the angels

The stable was that way

You told the shepherds

Not to leave their flock.

You showed the Wise Men

A different star

You booked

All the rooms

In every inn

And yet, in spite of this

The child was born

His glory shone

Both near and far

The Wise men found

That special star

The angels sang

The shepherds came

A promise made.

And though it's been

Two thousand year

We still greet this day

With cheer

And even you

Might shed a tear.

CATS

&

OTHER

CREATURES

"As every cat owner knows, nobody owns a cat."
Ellen Perry Berkeley

THE CAT DID IT

In my later years

I've come to see

The usefulness

Of a cat to me.

When there is

A mess in the house

I just have to say

To my nagging spouse

The cat did it.

When a nasty

Bill collector

Comes round

I just have to say

That bill

Can't be found.

The cat did it.

When dinner

Is late

And no one is fed

But you can find me

Asleep in my bed.

The cat did it.

When persons irate

Then turn on the cat

He looks at them

And squashes them flat.

I shrug my shoulders

What can I do?

The cat is above

All this hullabaloo.

The cat did it.

THROW THE CAT
UNDER THE BUS

We were young and we were strong

And we could never do no wrong

We fought our battles true and just

We parried with a mighty thrust

We never doubted we were right

We followed through with all our might

And if we ever had a doubt

We squashed it flat and threw it out

When it came down to blaming us

We'd throw the cat under the bus.

And now when age has slowed us down

We might remember with a frown

And see that we have come to know

The consequences that we sow

And recognize we may have erred

And just a little come aware

And teach our children so they see

There is a better way to be

But they can always give the blame to us

Just throw the cats under the bus.

RE-EDUCATING THE CAT 16 JUL 2022

The cat lies across his placemat

As he's about to put his plate down

He puts the cat on the floor

And turns to his seat

The cat's already sleeping there

Again, he throws it to the ground.

"I must re-educate the cat," he says.

(Oh, this I must see!)

He says he's done it now

He brings his plate, no cat

He sits upon his chair, no cat

The cat is sleeping peacefully

I think the education worked!

He starts to eat his dinner

The cat's eyes open

Slowly the cat gets up and walks toward him

The cat walks right under his chin

And over his plate not stepping on food

And waves his tail right under his nose

The cat turns and sits by him

Asking to be petted

He pets him, the cat purrs

"You did a wonderful job

Of re-education," I say

The cat looks at me as if to say

"We understand each other, sister."

THESE CATS

The house isn't large

But there's plenty of space

The cats even so stay

Right in your face.

The cat's in my chair

When I come to sit down

His head in the air

He makes not a sound

He jumps on the table

Making a stand

And wraps his tail

Round the nose

Of my man.

They're ready to rumble

They go nose to nose

Then all of a sudden

They're licking their toes.

A meow to tell me

He wants to go out

I open the door

He's out and about.

These cats they are winsome

And nasty and gay

They're cunning and feisty

And always at play.

Their presence has added

A sense to my life

That all is not only

A struggle and strife.

A MURDER OF CROWS   3 FEB 2022

A murder of crows

This morning

Blackening the trees

I thought some trucks

Were rumbling the street

Then I looked up to see

A mob of crows all cawing

In one cacophonous voice

Was this a gathering of protest

An expression of a grievance?

What made them

Come together?

A grievous day

In the world of crows?

How little do we know

This world we share.

I don't dispute you

Or your right to gather

I'm just passing by

But now I truly know

Why a group of crows

Is called a murder.

Seatt[le]

POST-INT[elligencer]

SEATTLE

OL. XVI.

OST-INTELLIGENCER.

HEADQUARTERS—Cor. Fourth
bia streets.

BY MAIL:

w advance......	$10 00
" in advance......	1 00
" in advance......	2 00
hs, in advance......	1 25
in advance......	2 00
ay, 1 year, in adv'ce	8 50
ER (in the city.)	
...... 25 cents

DAY, JUNE 7, 1889.

FIRE.

is told this morn-
tion. Our whole
rcial district, the
of the city, up-
business build-
glowing heap
nportant busi-
block, is left
very whole-
very news-
y store has

A SEA OF FIR[E]

The Business Part o[f] Seattle in Ruins.

Sixty-Four Acres o[f] Ground Swept.

Thirty-Two Blocks o[f] Smoking Debris

March 3, 1885:

Big Future Seen For S

The valley of the Skagit country, has in
destined to be one spects been follo
detriment of th

ELLIGEN

SHINGTON, FRIDAY, JUNE 7, 1889.

to stand in front of the wall of fire to
on the opera house. The whole
k of wooden buildings north of the
house, had by this time shared the
ral fate and were fast disappearing in
nd smoke. Virtually nothing could
one toward saving the opera house.
tried to brave the intense heat from
urning row across the street, but were
n back with scorched faces and
ing garments. The very hose melted
the firemen were forced to drag it
and reach the fire from Second street.

CONTROLLING THE MOB.

to this time Marshal Murphy had
the
Mayor
appeared on the scene and attempted
ring order
organi
ings in the path of the flames and the
streets in a few minutes were blocked
merchandise. Chief Butterfield
e in over 100 deputies and instructed
to arrest every man found steal-

which could be removed befor
reached. Boyd's photograph
the opposite corner, was nex
The buildings in this block—
Pacific Land Company's offic
hotel and the building occ
Congress saloon, were swept

SAVING THE BOSTON

The Boston block, oppo
lery, one of the finest struct
was in imminent danger
the window frames being
timely assistance of a
tators prevented destruct
formed—
to the fo
other reaching across U
the side entrance to th
caught fro
tructure occ
wards, which was de
dows in the front we
the plastering somewh
The structure would u
consumed if the bu
ed, as th
ent were now
aving the Front st
The Colonial bloc
Second and Colum
several times, but
the brigade was s
and the building
save the floodin

THE WORLD OUTSIDE
CURRENT EVENTS

"If more politicians knew poetry, and more poets knew
politics, I am convinced the world would be
a better place in which to live."

John Fitzgerald Kennedy

We were taking the bus

My first time

I was all keyed up

As only a little girl can be

While my Mom paid

I walked down the aisle

I saw two lovely seats in the back

"Come back here!" she called

We couldn't sit there

We had to sit in the front

I wanted to sit in the back

But it wasn't allowed

"Why not?" she wouldn't say

A little black girl got on

She and her Mom sat in my seats

"Mama look!" I cried

Mama just stared ahead, "Shush!"

Adult rules, I guess

They never make any sense.

It wasn't fair to me

It wasn't fair to the little black girl

Just not fair!

Soon we were there,

We got off the bus

Years later I read

About Rosa Parks

Shoot! I said, "That's us!"

But no one will celebrate

The little white girl

Who wanted to sit

At the back of the bus.

As everyone watched

Right on the tele

America got punched

Below the belly

Out of the shock

and the horror

The grief and the fear

An awesome new bloom

Began to appear

Flags hung out of windows

They hung upon doors

They flew from the buses

They flew above stores

They hung on the cars

They hung out of bars

A million plus flags

Saying, "This land is ours!"

When I remember what happened

That day

I'll always recall

The vigilant way

Those flags proudly wave

America, still

The Home of the Brave

The land of free will.

Whatever you say

It's apparent to me

America still

Is the Land of the Free.

A DOG AND PONY SHOW

A dog and pony show

It's a circus

It's fun, right?

And Cracker Jacks!

A dog and pony show?

TV news though

No prize in the box

A dog and pony show

Congress in session

Where's the cotton candy?

Reading the news

In a land far away

One country invaded

Another

Nothing to do

With me

I wondered

Is that what it was like

In 1939

When Hitler invaded

Poland?

Did Americans feel

Nothing to do

With us?

And yet it would

Have a lot

To do with us

Will this one

As well?

In truth

This planet

Is a ball

It has no sides

It all has everything

To do with

everyone

As we ride together

round the sun

Jesus said

You'll rise again.

Buddha said

You can transcend.

Jews awaiting

Their messiah,

Muslims strive

To live in Allah,

To Hindus what you sow

You reap

Your crime today

Will make you weep.

The truth you find

In all of these

Man knows the truth

When it he sees.

LOVE

(of course, what else?)

"At the touch of love, everyone becomes a poet."

Plato

PHYSICS VS. CHEMISTRY   8 SEP 2017

They say it's chemistry

I can't agree

Cause it's the physics

That really gets me.

Across the room you looked at me

An electric dart

Right through my heart

That was no chemical reaction

That was positive attraction!

It may not be well known

I'm sure I'm not alone

To have a back-up plan.

One true love for our life

In pleasure and in strife

Is what we understand.

But life can play its tricks

And when you're in a fix

You need a back-up plan.

And thus, when me you view

Alone with someone new

He's just my back-up plan.

Do you remember? I asked,

That night

we watched the moon,

Full and bright

in a clear cold night?

It was your birthday,

December,

Do you remember?

Yes, you said.

One word.

But I heard.

You remember

We remember

That December.

We watched the moon that night

 Full and streaming silver light

We watched as ones in tune

And sighed.

And after we had parted

We looked up heavy hearted

We watched each one alone

And sighed.

I watched outside my door

You watched from where you were.

We watched alone as one

And sighed.

The moon ignored our plight

But gave us each its light

We watched it both unknown

And sighed.

THE PROMISE

He made a promise on his part

He made it strong to me and true

Against the day it could come through

I hold his promise in my heart

I hold it close and oh so dear

And pray the day it's due draws near

CRAZY 21 APR 2019

I have a special kind of crazy for you:

Crazy about you

Crazy without you

Crazy to believe

Crazy not to grieve

Crazy in my head

Crazy in my bed

Crazy in my dreams

Crazy as it seems

This crazy doesn't go

I'm crazy.

Yes,

I know.

A MAD WOMAN LOVES YOU   4 FEB 2020

I have to call it the way that it's seen

I have to tell you it's not what I mean

A mad woman loves you that's all I can say

A mad woman loves you much better each day

Think you can handle this love that she's got?

Think you can tell her you'll give it a shot?

A mad woman loves you so give it a go

A mad woman loves you you're better off so.

BILL

But for you

I'd never know that

Love so true

Learns to grow

Hand in hand

Arm in arm

Cheek to cheek

All ways

To speak

Of being together

Me and you

You and me

This is how

I pray

We'll be

Together.

Now is come

The day is here

All I want is at my door

Open my arms

Open my heart

Let him in

This is the way love is

This is the way joy is

Now

With you.

A LOVE SONG

I never walk alone

You are everywhere

You're in my heart

You're in my mind

I see the world through you

I never walk alone

You're always by my side

Your presence is so true

I feel you with each breath

I feel the world through you

Some would say I'm haunted

Some call me obsessed

But I am never daunted

I chose you from the rest

I never walk alone

You're always In my mind

When I look I see you

I listen and I hear you

I live the world through you

TEXT 26/6/20 6:07 AM

My dear!

You are there

I am here

Delayed by a hurricane in Tampa

Landed in a thunderstorm in Denver

Flew into a heat wave in Portland

Tossed it off, no matter

Just had to get home to you.

To be with you

There is no not to be

No choice or either/or

No question or decision

There's only ever more.

You ask me

what I want or need

The answer is quite clear

To be with you

And then proceed

Through this and every year.

Just a taste on the lip

Not more than a sip

It opened a door

I hungered for more

It turned me around

Could not stand my ground

My when and my where

My what and my who

All spun around

And away they all flew

I had to re-order

Myself all anew

As if puzzle pieces

Had all blown apart

Put back together

Created new art.

My All,

My every,

My only one, too

My laughter,

My lover,

My dream that came true.

My instinct,

My wonder,

My thought in a jar,

My nearest,

My dearest,

My never too far

My truest,

My newest,

My luckiest win,

My torment,

My lament,

My secretest sin.

You asked me

To tell you

What you

Mean to me.

I've listed it here

In this panoply

A listing

Of all

The ways

 I hold

You dear.

Given to you

Without

Any fear.

Hopelessly

Helplessly

Fallen for you

Longing

To feel you

Never

To see you

Waiting

For someday

My wish

To come true

Hopelessly

Helplessly

In your embrace

Wishes

Can happen

In their

Own place.

My shameless heart

Does not as ought

But ventures out

Without a thought

Just sees your face

And is undone

Declares you are

Its only one.

I cannot change

Its choice you see

You're now the only

One for me.

My shameless heart

I curb it not

But feel the love

That it has wrought.

A HEART

I wear a heart

Upon my dress

Of gold or silver

(more or less)

My real heart

I've lost you see

You stole my heart

Away from me

I but wear

The symbol thus

To show my heart

Is placed in trust

I gave it to you

Willingly

And wear one here

For all to see.

WHEN WRONG BECAME
A RIGHT

When wrong became a right

Then sunshine shone all night

No trumpets blared before us

But songbirds in a chorus

Proclaimed the glowing sight

What was a wrong is now a right.

When it was wrong we walked away

To leave it for some other day

To never even look that way

So it would not destroy us.

Now we come with open heart

For what is right we make a start

To live the life before us.

When wrong became a right

We found our future bright

And all the world was for us.

This is a man who doesn't say

I love you very often

He doesn't have to say it

I know he does

This is a man who has loved me

For thirty years

But only told me he did last year

This is a man who waited for me

For ten years

Not seeing any other woman

This is a man who left

All his friends

And business connections

Put everything he owned

(Including two cats)

In his old truck

And drove 1000 miles

To be with me

This is a man who

Makes me breakfast every day

And kisses me good-by

When I leave in the morning

This is a man who hates Christmas

But helps me decorate

Because I love it

This is a man

Who reads my poems

And tells me to publish them

Even though they

Are about him

This is a man who doesn't have to say

I love you

Because this is a man

Who lives it.

A SPOT IN YOUR HEART   8 JUL 2020

I've got a spot in your heart

It came to me in a thought

It makes me feel warm

That this is the norm

I just need to know

And tell me if so

Is this a transient thought

Or is this a permanent spot?

PUSHOVER

Your kiss did it to me

Way back when

I've been your pushover

Ever since then.

The touch of your hand

Is with me for life

You'll be my man

And I'll be your wife

TO BE WITH YOU 2   25 SEP 2022

All I want is to be with you

Be by your side the whole day through

Not asking for the moon or sun

Just asking you to be my one

You say you're not the best for me

But I can only disagree

The best of men will sometimes err

That you do, too, I couldn't care

You are the one I've always known

You are the one who takes me home.

COME HOME TO ME

Come home to me

I wait for your touch

I listen for your step

Come home to me

To my open arms

To my smiling face

Come home to me

Find peace

Be free

Home is just

You and me

THE YEAR ONE

A year of you

A year of us

A ride aboard

Our magic bus

A year of you

A year of me

A year in which

We got to be

A year of love

A year of life

A year of very

Little strife

And when I'm at

Saint Peter's door

He'll ask me what

I'm thankful for

I'll say that out

Of all the rest

This was the year

I loved the best.

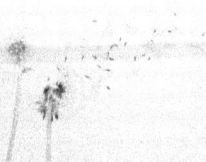

It's not that

Bad things aren't happening

In the world.

It's not that

Everything is perfectly

Fine.

It's not that all

My dreams have

Come true

The sun doesn't

Always shine

The skies aren't

Always blue.

It's just I'm

Living my life

With you.

You are present

In my space.

As I fall asleep

I notice

That there's

A smile

On my face.

DEATH & TIME

"Because I could not stop for Death
He kindly stopped for me
The carriage held but just ourselves
And immortality."

Emily Dickinson

DEATH

When I was young

Death and I had not met

Until I saw my grandmother

Released from pain

My grandfather reunited

With his sweet wife

Then I thought Death was kind

I saw him gently ease my sister

From her cancer ravaged body

And ease my husband also

From a life of pain

And now my friends and others too

It seems I've seen so many go

I stand here a witness

Death needs someone to know.

DEATH IS RUDE

Death is rude

He doesn't call

He doesn't knock

He doesn't call your secretary

For an appointment

He just comes in

At any time of day or night

Unannounced

If you are doing something

He doesn't care

You're done, son.

He snuffs you

Like a candle

You're out

No re-lighting

That candle

He doesn't take bribes

He doesn't bargain

If he's come for you

You're done

The end.

He ends things

And you're just one.

I wouldn't invite him

To my house.

He can't come

To my party.

AT THE MATCH BETWEEN
LOVE AND DEATH

"Love, you will find

Death is stronger

Than thee

No one can deny me

No one can get free

That beautiful woman

Who all men adore

Will one day be ashes

Her beauty no more

The mightiest man

With muscles and pride

Yet can't lift a hand

When Death's at his side

The king in his castle

With all of his gold

Is worth not a penny

When he's laid out cold

There's no one and nothing

Who won't fall to me

Thus, I am the winner

And ruler of thee."

Love smiled and looked

At Death in the eye.

"No, really there's no one

As mighty as I.

The Beauty, the Strongman,

The King all may die

Their love will live on

And always be nigh

Their love for a spouse,

For a child, for a friend

Nothing can stop it

From loving again."

"Curse you," said Death,

"I'm left at an end."

Love simply smiled

And held out his hand.

The crowd all cheered

From up in the stand.

PROVIDENCE

Every day I pass

The hospital where you died

I have to see it

As we go by

The last place

That I saw you

The last place

I talked to you

You'd think I'd

Not want to see

That last place

You were with me.

There's something

In its massive space

That makes me feel that

I can place

Some trust

In my remembrance

We were there

And you left me

And now I'm here

And all I see

Is Providence.

I died, but I came back,

You said.

Yes, you did, and we

Are glad.

Let's hope this lifetime

Breaks the chain,

So you can go and

Come again

But now you'll know,

It's your say so.

(written on my 73rd birthday)

I've called Time a liar.

I've called Time a friend

I've called Time a healer

Who helps me to mend,

I've called Time a hero

Who vanquished a foe

I've called Time a villain

Who caused me great woe,

I've called Time a constant

Who constantly changes

I've called Time a nuisance

Who just disarranges

I've called Time many

A name, don't you see

He doesn't care what I call him

He's just going to be

He's Time and he's constant

As we move along

All I can do

Is write him this song.

For Tim

He flew the whirlybird

On countless adventures

Take-offs and landings

High in the air

Completing his mission

Each time.

Although he's been grounded

For many a year

Flying still lives in his soul

Now he's gone airborne

For one last time

Said good-by to his crew

And set out alone

He's soaring above

The earth and her problems

He's on an adventure

Like none he has done.

NORTH DAKOTA

"After nightfall, the Bad Lands seem to be stranger and wilder than ever, the silvery rays turning the country into a kind of grim fairy land."

Theodore Roosevelt

There's no smog in North Dakota

But there's lots of snow

The air is clean and ever clear

But it's twenty-one below

There's no snow in Florida

It's sunny all the while

But when you're on the river

Beware of crocodile

It's not so hot in Oregon

The rain keeps it all green

But all the rainy weather

Can make you feel so mean

No rain in California

No trouble staying dry

But living in a drought zone

Can make things go awry

And thus each place

Has got its perks

Just find the one

For you that works.

My herd was a mighty one

Covering the plain

My size and my mightiness

Were all to my gain

But all of it lost

To these little men

Now it will never

Be so again

Your size and your numbers

Can all be undone

When faced with a man

And the force of his gun.

THE TIPSY BEAVER BAR   MAY 2022

Let's raise a glass

At the Tipsy Beaver Bar

To the men of the old

To the men who now are

Here's to the women who loved them

And the ladies who shunned them

Here's to the boy and here's to the girl

Here's to the ones who gave them a twirl

Here's to the papa's and mama's

The grampa's and grandma's

Here's to the best

And here's to the worst

Here's to the answer

To handle your thirst

And here's to the men

Of the Tipsy Beaver bar

The best of the rest

If ever there are!

He's weathered

Like an old cabin

That's seen the

Snow and the rain

Like a man

Who's been through it

Again and again

Like the tar

And the shingles

On top of the roof

One look at his face

Will show you the proof

He's seen it,

He's lived it

And everything too

Whatever comes up

He'll know what to do.

COWBOY

MAY 2022

He calls himself

A cowboy

I thought it a gag

But really he just

Hadn't wanted

To brag.

He rode in a rodeo

He rode on a bull

Okay he was just

A boy in a school

But he's more

Of a cowboy

Than I ever knew.

So Yippee Kai Yay

And one big yahoo!

BAD RIVER BLUES   MAY 2022

Got those Bad River blues

Ain't got no clues

To why I'm so down.

On a Bad River day

You walked away

With never a sound.

The Bad River flows

And tumbles my woes

Over the ground.

Bad River tell me

Wherever is he

No more around.

Bad River I plea

Wash over me

My sorrows to drown.

Drowning in fire

Can't get a breath

Down Firelake road

Feeling like death.

Lake water alone

Can't put out the fire

Sane thinking alone

Can't stop desire

Not a lake for floating

It's one for diving

Not a lake for going

It's one for arriving

Going ever deeper

Down and down

Happens every time

That you're around

If it's my time now

To truly expire

I might as well go

By water and fire.

A bad boy

In the badlands

Without a compass

A bad boy

In the badlands

Life moving too fast

So much trouble

You can get into

No one here

That you can turn to

The trouble you can find

All on your own

The trouble that finds you

When you're alone.

My bad boy

In the badlands

Please don't be lost.

My bad boy

In the badlands

Give me your trust.

Bad boy you can follow

This path to be free

Bad boy you can still

Be all you can be.

I didn't expect to see

Cacti in Canada

But there they are

A huge eclectic collection

Many varieties

Some are thirty feet tall!

We get a tour

Their caretakers

Showing them off

I look and suddenly

I know

These are alien to our planet

Brought here untold times ago

"You aren't from around here

Are you?"

I whisper to the plants.

A sudden hush, an expectancy

Fills the room.

"I'm not the one." I say.

I barely hear a sigh

As I turn and walk away.

An Earth girl,

I go to the gift shop

And buy a t-shirt.

THE ARTIST

"Fill your paper
with the breathing
of your heart."

William Wordsworth

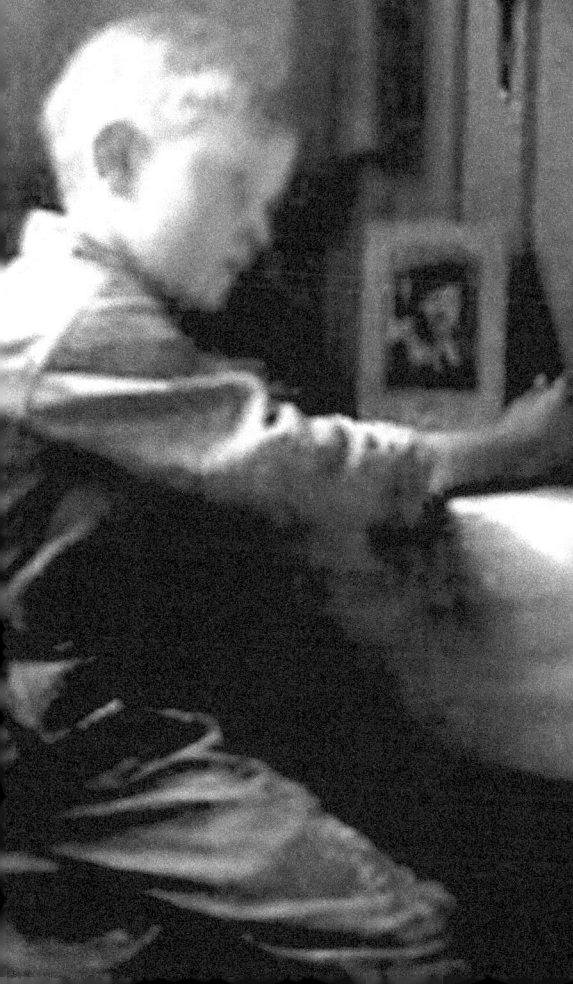

IN THE PLAYGROUND
OF MY MIND

In the playground of my mind

My pictures play with facts and thoughts

They mix it up and redefine

Imagination calls the shots,

The learned lessons fall away

No longer bound by reason

Here no one says you've gone astray

The snow can fall in any season.

Laughter peals at every hand

Shouts of joy are often found

A new beginning on demand

My thoughts fly upward all unbound.

CRAZY QUILT

A crazy quilt I imagine

Was first made on a cold night

When a mother had no time

To cut out and piece a true design

She had to keep her babies warm

Quickly she grabbed the scraps

She had on hand

Stitching then together

Without a plan

Covered her children on the bed

Where they slept sound.

Just so I write a poem

Taking the memories, ideas

And dreams in my heart

Stitching them together

Without a plan

That everyone who reads it

Will feel warm.

Sometimes it's fun

To put words together

To just watch them run

Without any tether

Their meaning

Is second

To the way that they sound

Their turnings and yearnings

Just fooling around.

You ask what I meant

When I wrote down

This song.

I wrote them

To hear them

Roll off my tongue.

IMAGINATION

What I imagine

I can see

What I think of

I can be

My mind can take

The darkest day

And make it shine

In bright array

No matter what

I won't be lost

Imagination

Is the boss!

WHY I WRITE

You ask why I write

I ask why you breathe

Both questions

Are the same

I breathe to live you say

And thus I write

As air is to the lungs

So verse is to the soul

I breathe deeply

And I sing.

As I rise

In early morn

A blank page

Looks at me

With scorn.

Some writer you are

Sitting there

With ne'er an idea

Anywhere

It taunts me

With its emptiness

It dares me

Not to make a mess

Let's see you

Come up with

A verse

I'm daring you

To do

Your worst

I cannot

Resist a dare

The words go

Flying

Through the air.

Take that

And that

I say in rage

And all my words

Fill up the page.

AND EVERYTHING ELSE

"Everything you can imagine is real.

Pablo Picasso

SUICIDE NOTE 18 JAN 22

Don't think about me

You'll be fine

Be sure the fault

Was only mine

Don't worry over

What you said

Be sure the fault

Was in my head

Don't linger

As they lay me down

No reason you should

Stick around

I don't need you

Any more

I am going through a door

At last, I truly get away

And there is nothing

You can say.

LEAVING

I'm leaving

And nobody wants me to go

The fact that they don't

Is sure nice to know.

I'm leaving

And really

I'm way overdue

I should have left sooner

When I was through

But the thrill of the journey

The fun of the game

Kept me still going

For more of the same.

But now I am leaving

And I say farewell

Remember me kindly

We played for a spell

And when we all gather

In some newer time

I'll still be there for you

We'll make a new rhyme.

HE DIDN'T AGREE   9 MARCH 2022

He never, but never

Had learned to agree

That surely, oh surely

is why he stayed free.

His mother and father

Said to him, Son

The way you are living

Will get you undone

His teachers and doctors

The delivery man

All said "Look here boy

You must do what you can,

You never just never

Should say what you saw

For surely, oh surely

That will break the law."

He never, but never

Could ever agree

And surely, oh surely

That's why he stayed free.

NOW I AM SEVENTY-THREE   10 FEB 2022

(after rereading Now We Are Six by

A. A. Milne)

Once I was nine

And feeling just fine

But now I am seventy-three

Once I could play

And have fun all day

But now I have places to be.

Once I had milk

And drinks of that ilk

But now I have chamomile tea

Once I had pets

And visits to vets

But now I have cats on TV

Once I could run

And had lots of fun

But now I have pain in my knee

Once I was young

My life had begun

But now it is starting to flee

I can look back

And see my own track

That got me to here don't you see

Once I was twenty

With time all aplenty

But now I am Seventy-three

SNOW IN APRIL

Stuck on the bus

Snow in April

Almost a crime

Out of time

Out of place

Another case

Of life not caring

About my pace

What I have planned

Must wait

I contemplate

The beauty of snow

Although I know

I will be late.

FEELING SAD

A sadness haunts me

Like a whisper

A fragment of some

Loss unknown

Perhaps to come

No reason for this shown

Is it a shadow

Of what is to be?

A sadness haunts me

For what

I dare not see.

RELATIVITY

The light I am

The light I was

The light that I will be

Einstein said

He couldn't know

Every bit of truth

Indeed for

What he knew

Was only

What he thought

But what he thought

Became reality for all

And what it brought

Became what's real.

Thus, everyone should

Think their truth

And base their life

On what they feel.

Big dreams

Fantastic structures

Amazing art

Conceived, planned

Seemingly obtainable

If I just can keep up

But my energy flags

My arms tire

My legs give out

My knees complain

I must sleep and eat

It seems

The body makes it's needs

Too well known

And I can't quite reach

The goals I'd seen

I falter, I fall

Just another

Victim of

Biology.

TAKING A WALK

The flowers

And the wood

Seen in my neighborhood

The trees

In autumn leaf

All add to

My belief

That while

Time's a thief

Still

God is good.

EYES SMILE

I never knew eyes smile

They laugh and frown

In fact, less guarded

Than the whole face

Which often wears a mask

And hides a true intent

Behind a grin.

Eyes speak if we but look

And not depend on sound.

GLASSES

"Mama! I can see!

Every leaf on every tree!"

I never even knew

A sharp, distinct view

Was possible

I was twelve when

This was revealed

I've seen this way since

Through changing lenses

As age again blurred my senses.

But what lens can see the soul?

Can separate the sections

From the whole?

Can bridge the distance in the mind?

And point us where to find

The realest truest view?

One must open the mind's eye

And peer myopically at first

Until one sees

The colors and the lines

And all that defines

That which is.

LAST MAN STANDING

I have been

Battered by the storm

Tumbled by the waves

Rocked by the earth

Lied to and about by cohorts

Betrayed by other people

Abandoned by friends

Deceived by leaders

And I have watched

Storms subside

Waves go calm

Earth get steady

Cohorts die

People discredited

Friends return

Leaders defeated.

I still stand

Still my own man,

A witness and a warning.

When it's all over

When all has been said

When all has been done

At the final end of everything

What will be true my dear

Is it was you my dear

Who made my soul sing.

Miss Peterson is of Swedish-Italian descent which makes it difficult for her to maintain a proper balance. She has inherited some of her skill from the only published poet in her family-King Charles I-whose poem was written on the eve of his execution for treason.

Of her childhood she says, "I was born on St. Stephen's Day (you remember St. Stephen, he was the one who was stoned.) About her childhood she says, "I was an imaginative, bossy, fearful, little girl and my childhood was full of small traumas. I am happy to say that this has changed and they are now larger. I was raised on fairy tales and musical comedies, which is why I write so many whimsical comic poems."

Her favorite authors and poetic influences she lists as Cummings, Shakespeare, Thomas, Roethke, Levertov and Blake. The most apt description of her would be "serious and sincere", also honest, aggressive, intense and neurotic.

Speaking of her keen poet's eye, she has commented, "I am near-sighted."

Miss Peterson plans to spend the next five years at Antioch College as poet-in-residence on a special grant. Although this is her first book, Miss Peterson had had individual pieces published in The Lab Writer, La Douce Vie, and Unitarian Quarterly. Next time she hopes to get paid.

Ms Negley was born in Chicago and raised in the South and the West Coast. She spent most of her adult life in San Francisco where she married and raised two children. In 2016, she and her husband moved to Beaverton, Oregon to be near their grandchildren and she lives there today. She is an ordained minister and has spent most of her life helping people with spiritual counseling.

Ms. Negley wrote her first poem at the age of 4 and has continued to write all her life. She published her first book of poems, *The Heart Has No Rules,* in 2021. She lives with her second husband and his two cats. They are Vegas cats and not too fond of her but she has recently been promoted to "Chief Door Opener." She feels that she is getting somewhere with them.